DRAZEN PETROVIC

KENNY ANDERSON

RICK BARRY

STEPHON MARBURY

JULIUS ERVING

JAYSON WILLIAMS

BERNARD KING

DERRICK COLEMAN

KEITH VAN HORN

BILL MELCHIONNI

KENYON MARTIN

BUCK WILLIAMS

CREATIVE C EDUCATION
MICHAEL E. GOODMAN

Published by Creative Education, 123 South Broad Street, Mankato, MN 56001

Creative Education is an imprint of The Creative Company.

Designed by Rita Marshall

Photos by Allsport, NBA Photos, SportsChrome, Brian Spurlock

Library of Congress Cataloging-in-Publication Data

Goodman, Michael E. The history of the New Jersey Nets / by Michael E. Goodman.

p. cm. — (Pro basketball today)   ISBN 1-58341-106-2

1. New Jersey Nets (Basketball team)—

Juvenile literature. [1. New Jersey Nets (Basketball team)—History.

2. Basketball—History.] I. Title. II. Series.

GV885.52.N37 G66 2001   796.323'64'0974941—dc21   00-047330

First Edition 9 8 7 6 5 4 3 2 1

NEW JERSEY IS A STATE OF GREAT VARIETY. WITH ITS NORTHERN TIP NEAR NEW YORK CITY AND ITS SOUTHERN

tip near Philadelphia, much of the state is comprised of urban and sub-

urban communities. In addition, many of America's biggest corporations

5

call New Jersey home. Yet the state is also famous for its scenic farming

regions, which have inspired its nickname—the "Garden State."

Up until the late 1960s, basketball fans in New Jersey split their

allegiance. Some rooted for the Knicks in New York, and others cheered

for the Warriors and then the 76ers in Philadelphia. Finally, in 1967,

New Jersey got its own franchise in the American Basketball Association

WALT SIMON

(ABA). That club—called the Nets—eventually joined the National Basketball Association (NBA) in 1977.

{EARLY DAYS IN THE ABA} When the ABA was formed in February 1967, the league had high hopes but not much cash. That meant that ABA teams often played in low-rent arenas and featured second-level talent compared to the NBA. A club called the New Jersey

6   Americans was one of the original members of the ABA. The Americans played their home games in Teaneck in a gloomy U.S. military building called the Teaneck Armory. The building's roof leaked, and one home game even had to be postponed because of rain. Still, the Americans finished their first season a respectable 36–42.

The next season, the Americans had a new home and a new name. They relocated to New York's Long Island and became known as the

KENDALL GILL

Rick Barry scored at a blistering pace throughout the early **1970s**.

RICK BARRY

New York Nets. The team's management hoped the changes would lead to greater success for the franchise, but it didn't work out that way. The Nets suffered through a disappointing 17–61 season that year, and fewer than 1,000 people showed up to see most of the club's home games.

Then, in 1969, a wealthy businessman named Roy Boe stepped in. Boe bought the team and convinced two young and talented NBA players—guard Bill Melchionni and forward Sonny Dove—to jump to his ABA squad. The two newcomers teamed up with the Nets' best veteran, Levern Tart, to form the nucleus of an exciting and much-improved team.

Things got even better for the Nets during the 1970–71 season, when former NBA scoring champ Rick Barry joined the team. Barry was an offensive machine. The lanky forward could hit long-range jumpers or

Guard Bill Melchionni led the ABA in assists in **1970–71**, dishing out eight per game.

9

BILL MELCHIONNI

Like Rick Barry before him, forward Keith Van Horn was an offensive force.

KEITH VAN HORN

drive to the hoop with equal success. He also knocked down more than

90 percent of his free throws, tossing the ball up with an old-fashioned,

underhand shooting style. "I think Rick Barry is the

greatest and most productive offensive forward ever to

play the game," said Bill Sharman, Barry's former coach

with the San Francisco Warriors.

In his first year with New York, Barry rang up an

Billy Paultz
set a
rebounding
standard later
aspired to
by fellow
center Evan
Eschmeyer.

12   average of 29 points per game and became the first Nets player named

to the ABA's All-League team. He upped his scoring average to 31 points

per game the next year—second-best in the league. Barry, along with

Melchionni, center Billy "the Whopper" Paultz, forward Manny Leaks,

and guard John Roche, helped the Nets post a winning record for the

first time in 1971–72. The club even reached the final round of the ABA

playoffs that year before losing the championship to the Indiana Pacers.

BILLY PAULTZ

{THE DOCTOR IS IN THE HOUSE} The Nets quickly fell

toward the bottom of the league standings again in 1972–73 after a

judge ruled that Barry had to return to his old NBA club, the Warriors.

That left the Nets without a leader—but not for long. The next year,

Roy Boe traded for superstar Julius Erving, giving the Nets one of the

ABA's most spectacular scorers.

Erving was nicknamed "Dr. J" for the way he "operated" on the

court. The 6-foot-6 forward moved with astonishing speed and grace,

Julius Erving, Billy Paultz, and forward Larry Kenon all played in the **1974** ABA All-Star Game.

and his soaring dunks filled sports highlight films. When

he jumped, he seemed to defy gravity, maneuvering in

space and sailing over opponents much like Michael

Jordan did years later. "Doc goes up and never comes

down," said astonished teammate Bill Melchionni.

The Nets didn't come down either during the 1973–74 season,

Dr. J's first with the club. They won 55 regular-season games, 25 more

than the previous year. To top off the year, the Nets routed the Utah

Stars in the league finals to win their first ABA championship, and Dr. J

earned his own title—ABA Most Valuable Player.

Two seasons later, the Nets staged a replay of that magical year.

They duplicated their 55–29 record, Dr. J again led the league in scoring

JULIUS ERVING

with an average of 29 points per game, and New York romped to its sec-

ond ABA championship.

{JERSEY-BOUND} The big story of the 1975–76 season wasn't

the Nets' success, however. That year also marked the end of the ABA's

brief history. The ABA and NBA merged in early 1976, and four ABA

franchises—the Indiana Pacers, Denver Nuggets, San Antonio Spurs, and

New York Nets—joined the bigger and older league.

Nets fans were thrilled that their team was joining the NBA, but

their excitement was short-lived. They soon learned that

Julius Erving was involved in a contract dispute with Roy

Boe, who refused to pay his star more money. In the end,

Boe traded Dr. J to the Philadelphia 76ers for players and

cash. "How could anyone do this to us?" wondered Nets

guard John Williamson. "Our season is over already." Williamson turned

out to be right. The club plummeted in 1976–77, compiling an NBA-

worst 22–60 record.

Before the next season, Boe moved the Nets back to their first

home state, and in September 1977, the New Jersey Nets were officially

born. Along with its new home, the team also acquired a new offensive

star—rookie sensation Bernard King, a Brooklyn native. That first year,

Guard John Williamson's scoring heroics took center stage in the Nets' first seasons in New Jersey.

JOHN WILLIAMSON

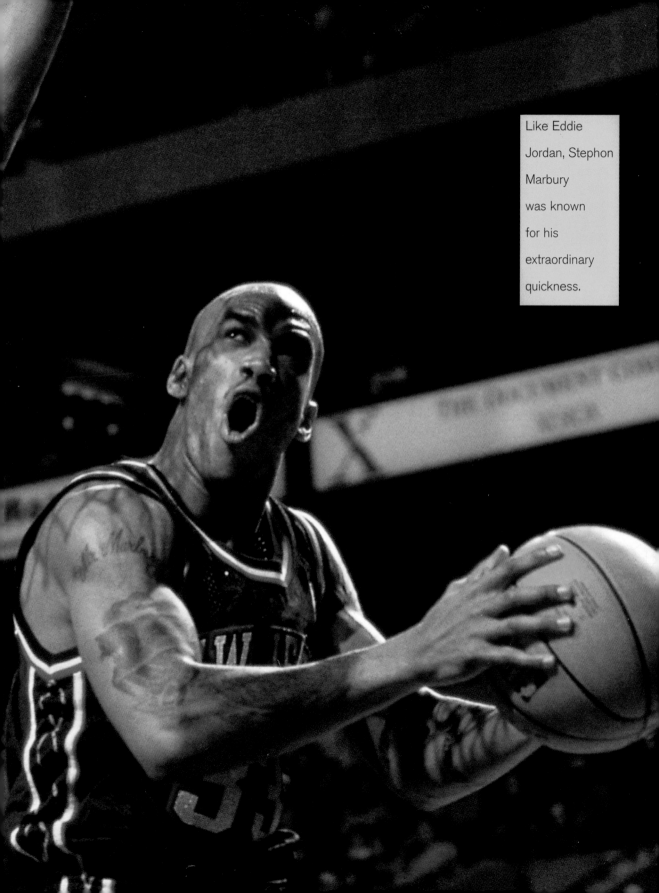

Like Eddie Jordan, Stephon Marbury was known for his extraordinary quickness.

the exciting young forward averaged 24 points and 9 rebounds a game.

"Bernard King is a scoring machine," said Red Holzman, a former Knicks

coach. "What impresses me is how he shoots with such

quickness and accuracy. Other teams overplay him and

try to deny him the ball, but he keeps scoring."

During the Nets' first years in New Jersey, the nucle-

us of King, shot-blocking wizard George Johnson, guards

John Williamson and "Fast Eddie" Jordan, and defensive forward Jan

van Breda Kolff kept the Nets near the middle of the NBA standings.

Then injuries took their toll, and the club dropped back to the bottom

of the pack. Soon King and several other stars were traded away and

replaced by inexperienced youngsters such as guard Darwin Cook, cen-

ter Mike Gminski, and forwards Mike O'Koren and Cliff Robinson as

the Nets tried to rebuild.

Bernard King
tied a
New Jersey
record by
pouring in
44 points
in one game
in **1977–78**.

BERNARD KING

{THE "BUCK" STOPS HERE} As the Nets entered the 1980s,

New Jersey management turned to veteran NBA coach Larry Brown and

asked him to turn the franchise around. Brown got right to work. His

first move was to select 21-year-old power forward Charles "Buck"

Williams in the 1981 NBA Draft. Williams gave the team ferocious

rebounding and a solid inside scoring touch, abilities that earned him the NBA's coveted Rookie of the Year award after the 1981–82 season.

"Every team should be blessed with a Buck Williams," said former Nets

Center Darryl star Rick Barry, then an NBA television analyst. "He's

Dawkins, best

known for his consistent, hardworking, and tough."

thunderous

dunks, Brown combined Buck Williams with a backcourt of

rejected 152 Ray Williams and Otis Birdsong, center Darryl Dawkins,

shots in

1982–83. and sharpshooting forward Albert King (Bernard's

22 younger brother) to create a well-balanced unit. The former cellar-

dweller Nets rose among the NBA's elite teams with a 49–33 record in

1982–83. Everything was looking up in New Jersey until the last two

weeks of the season, when Coach Brown announced that he would be

leaving the team. The announcement seemed to deflate the young Nets,

who quickly bowed out of the playoffs.

The following year, new coach Stan Albeck added talented point

DARRYL DAWKINS

Buck Williams averaged 12 boards a game for seven straight seasons in the **'80s**.

BUCK WILLIAMS

guard Micheal Ray Richardson to the Nets' lineup. With Richardson on

board, the Nets not only earned a spot in the playoffs again, but they

pulled off a major upset by eliminating Julius Erving's

Philadelphia 76ers, the defending NBA champions, in an

exciting first-round matchup.

    After two more winning seasons, the club went on

an extended drought for the rest of the 1980s. They

Defensive standout Mookie Blaylock racked up a team-high 169 steals in **1990–91**.

failed to make the playoffs five years in a row, despite the efforts of

solid performers such as guards Lester Conner, Dennis Hopson, and

Mookie Blaylock, centers Sam Bowie and Chris Dudley, and forwards

Chris Morris and Roy Hinson. The club reached its low point when it

struggled to a franchise-worst 17–65 record in 1989–90.

    {REBUILDING IN THE 1990s} The Nets' turnaround in the

early 1990s was fueled by two top draft picks: power forward Derrick

MOOKIE BLAYLOCK

Coleman and point guard Kenny Anderson. Both were exceptional but inconsistent talents. When he was motivated, Coleman could dominate games, hitting 18-foot jumpers with deadly accuracy or making daring

moves inside. Anderson was an outstanding passer and ranked near the top of the league each year in assists and steals, though he had a tendency to commit too many turnovers.

The talented duo, along with long-range bomber Drazen Petrovic from Croatia, powered the Nets to a 43–39 record in 1992–93, ending a seven-year streak of losing seasons. Then, in the summer of 1993, Petrovic was tragically killed in a car crash. The Nets were shocked by the loss of their friend and teammate, but they pulled together to finish the 1993–94 season at 45–37 and earned a matchup against the New York Knicks in the first round of the playoffs. The Nets had beaten their nearby rivals four times in five meetings during the season, but New York came out on top in the playoffs.

In **1993–94**, point guard Kenny Anderson became the Nets' first All-Star in nine seasons.

Beset by injuries the next year, the Nets fell below .500 again, and the team's management decided to clean house. Coleman was traded to the 76ers for 7-foot-6 center Shawn Bradley, Anderson was sent to Charlotte in exchange for swingman Kendall Gill, and point guard

KENNY ANDERSON

Chris Childs and power forward Jayson Williams were promoted to the starting lineup. Despite the changes, the Nets continued to struggle.

In **1997–98**, Jayson Williams ranked second in the NBA with nearly 14 boards a game.

Even the hiring of successful college coach John Calipari could not turn the Nets' fortunes around. Within two years, Calipari and several players were gone, and the Nets continued to look for a winning combination.

{STEPHON ON THE RUN} Still, all of the losing did

have one positive effect. The Nets were able to pick early in several consecutive drafts, bringing such talented newcomers as guard Kerry Kittles, forward Keith Van Horn, and center Evan Eschmeyer to New Jersey. Then, in a three-way trade with the Milwaukee Bucks and Minnesota Timberwolves in March 1999, the Nets acquired outstanding point guard Stephon Marbury.

At 6-foot-2 and 180 pounds, Marbury was a small man, but he was

JAYSON WILLIAMS

given a huge responsibility—making the New Jersey offense go. When former Los Angeles Lakers guard Byron Scott took over as the Nets' coach before the 2000–01 season, he immediately made clear the importance of Marbury's role. "I have to be in his head, and he has to be me out there on the floor," said Scott. "He's going to be the coach out there."

Marbury was not the only new Nets player that Coach Scott relied on to power New Jersey into the future. Another vital component was forward Kenyon Martin, whom the Nets selected with the top overall pick in the 2000 NBA Draft. Martin was a rugged player who loved to battle under the boards for rebounds and emphasized defense before offense. To prove the point, Martin chose six as his uniform number in honor of Bill Russell, one of the best defenders in NBA history.

Kerry Kittles connected on 40 percent of his shots from three-point range in **1999–00**.

KERRY KITTLES

Forward Aaron Williams emerged as a tough rebounder and defender in **2000–01**.

AARON WILLIAMS

With the addition of Kenyon Martin, the Nets were ready to rise in the standings.

KENYON MARTIN

Although they suffered some hard times during the 1990s, the

Nets are confident that their fortunes will soon change. "I've always

been a very lucky person," Coach Scott announced, "and I see our luck

changing here." With a desire for success and a little bit of luck, these

former champs of the ABA plan to soon conquer the NBA.